The First Nine Lives of Squeekie the Bookstore Cat

Squeekie the Bookstore Cat

Assisted by

Kristian Beverly

Samantha Coons

Michelle Haring

Katie Twigg

Copyright © 2016 Squeekie the Bookstore Cat

Second Edition Copyright © 2019

All rights reserved.

ISBN: 978-1-7331837-2-7

DEDICATION

To all my friends who have found their forever homes, and to those who are still seeking their family.

To my humans, both those who work in the bookstore and those that stop to pet me and tell me I'm pretty.

CONTENTS

    Acknowledgements   i

1. Squeekie and the Little Horses   1
   Kristian Beverly

2. Squeekie Finds Breen a Home   11
   Kristian Beverly

3. Squeekie and the Friends that Grow Up   21
   Kristian Beverly

4. Squeekie and the Kitten   27
   Samantha Coons

5. Squeekie and the Books   41
   Samantha Coons

6. Squeekie and Michelle   59
   Samantha Coons

7. Squeekie and the Ghosts   67
   Michelle Haring

8. Squeekie and Annika   83
   Michelle Haring

9. Squeekie and His Friends   93
   Katie Twigg

ACKNOWLEDGMENTS

I would like to thank all the makers of treats and good things to eat.

1

Squeekie and the Little Horses

Kristian Beverly

Cats were created with magic. Or so they were told. It was handed down through the litters born, a constant hum that told cats that they were special and that while they were capable of ruling the world, it was more fun to let others do it for them.

Magic flowed from their whiskers to their toes and through their tails. It was a soft magic instead of the loud dramatic variety. It allowed them to disappear and reappear without a sound. They could jump from high heights and land on their toes with only a mild soreness lingering. It allowed them to stay as they were, never bending to become different.

The only catch to the magic was following the rules.

The store was different, Squeekie thought.

Often Squeekie felt like the ruler of his bookstore. He remembered the tale of the first cats, adorned in golden jewelry and bowed to. It gave them the precision to jump and grab. To watch without having to move

He often felt like the ruler of his own castle with a revolving door of not subjects, but equals. Equals that always eventually found their own castle. Magic, the loud and dramatic type, called to Squeekie but he refused to answer it. He didn't like loud and dramatic unless it was his own voice. He talked to the ghosts when alone at night but always made sure he padded down the aisles, meowing to make sure the humans had left. He wasn't embarrassed of magic, he just didn't want to make it known in the way it could be. Cats were told the stories of their magic and the stories of fallen magic. Humans meant well with their hearts but power had the ability to corrupt and one of the most stark reminders of the whole ordeal was the platypus. What the creature originally looked like had been lost in translation, but the happily beaver duck creature was a reminder of magic gone wrong and forgotten. Especially the loud and dramatic kind. It spoke in screams instead of whispers. It broke doors instead of tapping. And it frightened him when he thought of what could happen, particularly at night.

Today was a new day, and one of the special humans had brought in a tote. Squeekie's tail curved over his back as he moved to smell it. It was different than books, even though he knew his pack of special humans spoke in books.

Today, however the tote was filled with horses. Plastic horses.

His special human held the horse figure, using her free hand to talk.

"See, you can show them and win ribbons," K said.

Two other special humans stood around the counter admiring the model and the case of ribbons K placed on the counter like a blanket.

"It's basically like an art show. You judge it as a moment along with the props and tack and placement," she continued.

Squeekie could smell the outdoors and the places the model had traveled to. He smelled the salt of the ocean and chili. He loved chili when he could steal it from humans.

His first special human smiled before saying, "Ready for the sale? Put them back here and we can go."

K lugged her tote around the piles of books

before placing them behind the counter.

The special humans worked in their own way, closing out and turning off the lights before scurrying out the door. Squeekie heard a car's engine rubble to life and watched the reflection of car lights bounce off of book cases.

He sat at the counter. The perfumes and smoke smells that humans wore had dissipated into the air as night worn on. The smell of trees, of dust, from the books filled the air. Annika, his love, hadn't talked to him in days and was still fuming in the back room, so Squeekie had the whole front of the store to himself.

The moon's light reflected into the store and the darkness of night created tall, warping shadows.

They normally didn't bother Squeekie, but the hum and pull of magic was more powerful tonight. It tickled the pads of his paws. He scratched and licked his feet but each lick left his mouth buzzing like the time he'd licked the hand of someone that held peppers all day.

Why—

Annika padded out of the back room, her fluffy tail twitching back and forth. She moved past Squeekie without a glance. Humans called them siblings, one with more fur than the other.

But weren't siblings supposed to act similarly? He and Annika did look similar in the way that crocodiles and alligators did. A part of the same mold with one or two features being telltale signs of why they weren't. Annika glared more than she looked while Squeekie purred more than she meowed. Her feet didn't seem to hurt. She didn't look behind or around herself.

Was he crazy?

Annika moved to the back of the counter and Squeekie turned to watch her. She moved to the plastic tub and nudged it with her nose. Annika's flat face pressed into it again, but the top didn't budge.

A growl rumbled in her throat. "Open it," Annika said.

She didn't add please or even look at Squeekie. Only demanded.

"No, they would be mad," Squeekie muttered.

The much smaller cat turned to face Squeekie. Her mouth was a permanent frown, but it didn't always reach her eyes. Today it did. "Don't care. Open it Squeekie."

Squeekie leapt down from the counter. K said she didn't clasp it closed because of fumes or air flow. It was important for the little plastic horses to get special airflow. Squeekie didn't understand how fake horses could breathe, but he'd learned humans had a funny way of caring for fake things.

Annika swiped her paw at Squeekie, catching him at his shoulder with her sharp claws. "Come on Squeekie, or else they'll suffocate!"

Squeekie wasn't sure who they was but he didn't want anyone dying on his watch. He pushed his nose against the top, sniffing it for a scent other than plastic and not finding any, opened it. Then he listened.

Tiny nickers and whinnies.

"Annika—" Squeekie started.

Annika stuck her face into the tub. She seemed fine with live little horses.

"You know this is the bad type of magic," Squeekie said.

Annika shook her head. Squeekie often wondered if the tiny head contained a brain or if it had all been wasted on beauty but it didn't matter right now.

Right now there were tiny creatures that weren't supposed to be moving.

"I want to do this type of magic. It actually does something," Annika said. "And yes, I've heard the stories. I don't care."

Squeekie hissed. It was a weird sound coming

from him, as if he rarely ever used it. Which he never did but it needed to be made. He wanted the magic out of his paws.

"How are you going to make this better by the morning?" Squeekie asked. "I doubt she'd be happy about it. You saw the ribbons."

Annika ignored him, her eyes bright as she watched the bubble wrap move.

He moved around the container, watching the bubble wrapped horses move like a wave. A small head popped out, and stared at him.

One tiny horse jumped out of the tub. Her face was small and refined. She stood about a eight inched high at her ears and she flicked her tail. "How?"

Squeekie sighed before sniffing her. "Magic."

The horse nodded like she understood. But how can one understand when they'd never been alive prior? How?

Squeekie grabbed a piece of bubble wrap with his mouth and pulled backwards, exposing more models. A herd of tiny horses.

They ran away from him in a herd. Annika padded next to Squeekie and yawned.

"You can't be tired," Squeekie snapped. "How are we going to fix this?"

Annika growled. "Doesn't matter. They're fine

and the magic will go down. All's good. Just don't eat them."

Squeekie leaned back. "Me? Eat them? Why would I do that?"

Annika swiped her tail back and forth. "You eat the kitten's food. You eat all of the treats. Why wouldn't you eat tiny horses?"

Squeekie walked away and sat down.

"Loosen up Squeekie," Annika purred. "This won't happen again."

The tiny horses came out again and Annika chased after them.

Squeekie paused before galloping after.

They ran and ran around the store, paws scraping where hooves had recently pounded. They didn't ask each other for names, because they would have had to stop and stopping meant recognizing that this would eventually end.

The horses climbed into the tub as the sun began to come up. Squeekie would not miss them in the way they were as a whole. He'd miss them individually though. The magic had dulled throughout the night, like it had finally let some of its build up simmer down to a manageable level. And the horses felt it. They walked with their heads and tails low, feet dragging behind, like they'd been given medicine.

It had been a full night, one that he'd miss but never wanted to participate in again.

"Will you miss being whole?" Squeekie asked.

The little Clydesdale stopped his walk and looked at Squeekie. His dark brown eyes seemed puzzled. "Why would you say that?"

"You can't move anymore."

"I think one night of this is enough to last my whole life." The horse said. "I never want to do this again."

Living would be hard if you spent your whole life stilled.

The next morning K walked in and nearly screamed. Why was the container to her models open? And how on earth were they positioned the way they were?

AUTHOR BIOGRAPHY

Kristian Beverly loves to write and has been writing her whole life. Before being able to write, she illustrated her stories but now write short fiction and novels. When not writing, Kristian can be found on the back of a horse, creating art, or reading.

2

Squeekie Finds Breen a Home

Kristian Beverly

Breen was the hardest of my friends to find a home for.

Out of all of the cats, and there had been plenty, Breen seemed to repel any sort of interest or human interaction that he could.

I liked to consider myself to be the best human finder on Earth. Okay, maybe not Earth, but from the select places I've been and people I've met, I felt my credentials were up to par with even the most seasoned human adopters. Squeekie, certified human finder. I'd be the leader of the club if cats roamed around the way humans did. But we didn't, and I'm president of the club even though the club members constantly change. I've had yet to meet or hear of a cat that'd found more humans for their friends than me. It was an attention to detail, a feeling deep in my gut that made me send my friend to those people. In most cases, even if it wasn't on that day or the next, eventually that human and friend found each other and lived happily ever after.

Well, except for Breen.

Picking a human was a large task. One that even kept the humans puzzled at times. In eleven months I hadn't felt an inkling for a human for Breen.

Today the store had been busy. I maneuvered through long, rotund, short legs, and wheels. People rubbed my fur as I arched my back. I answered them with long purring responses. But I'd been alone the whole time.

I loved humans, no matter how different each one looked. Cats had come through, some looking so alike that I'd call them by the wrong name. Even their smells were the same. My humans often complained about people caring about how different they were, but it was my favorite part about them.

Some cats loved to find their humans with minimal help from me. Others were next to me every step of the way, purring when I did, meowing or even reaching up and grabbing at legs to demand attention. I taught cats how to bargain for attention the way the special humans taught humans about books.

I scrunched up my nose and flagged my tail back and forth as I made my way towards the back room. People had asked for Breen today. I yowled for them to follow me to the special human curtains. It was in the back of the store, with a heavy covering in front of it. Only the special humans were supposed to go back there, but I bet they would have made an exception if Breen had found a human for himself. Just a peak would have shown my friend. Just one small glance.

Sure, it would have been going against the sign if I'd brought them with me, but I don't think anyone would have complained if it found Breen a new home.

But Breen had stayed hidden and asleep all day.

I padded through the entry way, the words at the tip of my tongue. I could yell at him and scare him into finding a person for himself. It sounded like a grand idea, one that maybe would force him to find someone for himself.

I stopped in front of the curtain, the colors a mix of grays and whites before crawling underneath and seeing the huge expanse of Breen.

Breen opened his eyes before sighing. He twitched his nose before curling backward and licking long fur.

Some humans said Breen and I looked alike, but I didn't see it. They said we were both sandy colored, which was true, but the similarities stopped there. Where I was lean and ready to run and chase after balls, Breen was a cylinder of fluff.

"It's hard to find a human," Breen said.

His tail was lowered and his eyes downcast. I moved towards him, letting him lean some of his weight on me. I turned my head and gave him a reassuring lick on his head.

"It can be, but you hiding won't ever work," I said.

"Why find a human when something bad could happen to them? That's what happened to my person, and I don't think I want to get another one."

I never pushed my friends to tell their stories. It wasn't mine to ask or tell. If a cat wanted to tell me their story they did. If not, they rewrote their life here. It was only fair.

We sat in front of the curtain, Breen's body

tense. His legs were as stiff as a stick and his fur stuck up on his back. He was poised to run, even though we were the only ones back here. The humans stood and talked amongst each other in the front room, and I wanted to join them, run through their legs and let them pet me. But I couldn't leave Breen. No matter how much I wanted to.

I nudged Breen with my paw, making him stand up.

It took a couple of days and much ankle biting to get Breen to make an appearance. He wasn't afraid of the people, just lackluster towards them.

"She reminds me of my first human," Breen said.

With sad eyes, he eyed a woman. The woman had sparse long hair that reminded me of dust, and her clothes were baggy, like a kitten's loose skin. Her back was bent in a permanent hook, but her eyes glittered when she saw us.

I watched as she grabbed my favorite box. Treats.

She shook it once, and I trotted to her. Breen followed.

The special humans were the only other ones

in the store, and it was quiet minus me crunching on the delicious treats. Any cat that didn't like treats weren't fully feline.

I wanted to rub against the woman's leg, but I was afraid of pushing her over. She seemed like string and so fragile. She smelled like sugar and flowers.

Breen rubbed against her and meowed.

She cooed, and her bony hand brushed against Breen's fur.

I sat near the counter and watched Breen and the woman.

"Oh, I used to have a pretty like you," she whispered. "I miss him."

Breen's tail flicked back and forth. "You look like my old human."

They kept as they were, the woman petting Breen and Breen peering up at the woman.

"Time to leave," a younger woman said.

She burst into the store, and her shoes clacked on the floor. She tossed her hair back and looked at the older woman.

"Doesn't this look like my Putter?" the older woman asked.

The younger girl had long and full hair, and the same face as the older one.

"Yes, it does," she said. "But Putter had to go

elsewhere when you went to the nursing home."

"Was she your human?" I asked Breen.

He still had that faraway look. The woman really liked Breen, but the younger one didn't seem to.

Breen shook his head. "Before I came here, my human's kitten put me in the carrier with my favorite blanket. My human had been having issues moving well, so they said she had to go away, but I couldn't come along. So they left me outside, and I couldn't get out. Some nice humans brought the carrier in but didn't know I was in there. I'd never been without my person before then, and then I never saw her again."

Breen stood up and began moving towards the back of the store. I followed, flicking my tail back and forth.

When we reached the door, Breen continued, "They noticed that the carrier was heavy and found me. There was a note attached, and they were really mad about it. But I don't blame my human, I just hope she's okay now."

"We can find you a human Breen," I said. "I'll help you find a second forever human."

Breen nodded his head. "I believe you Squeekie."

The days became weeks but didn't become months. Breen didn't want to weave through people's legs. He wanted to watch from above on the cat walk. He'd rather window shop for a human than let them pick, and I was by his side the whole time.

Holidays were busy. Particularly the week before Christmas.

Parents and children and people adorned with Reindeer hats and sweaters flooded the store with cheer. For once, Breen didn't want to climb the cat walk.

A family had walked in and smelled like cookies and gingerbread. I wished I loved the smell of those treats and of the holiday cheer, but they made me itch and want to sneeze. Breen however, loved it. He sniffed the air. "I like these humans."

I sat at the counter and watched Breen curl his tail over his back and meow.

The human kittens squealed before rubbing his coat. He buried himself into the great cat and Breen nudged his head against the little kid's side.

His parents glanced back at their son before moving through the shelves. Breen and the human kitten stayed with each other. When his parents returned, they found Breen curled in the little human kitten's lap. The adult humans paused and looked at Breen before looking at each other. The group of them sat down and Breen arched his back and rubbed hands with his head like he was already a part of the family.

It had taken a while for me to find a human for Breen, but I knew this was a forever one.

Squeekie the Bookstore Cat

3

Squeekie and the Friends that Grow Up

Kristian Beverly

Squeekie went around through each day trying to converse with people. Sometimes he wondered if the issue was that he didn't meow loud enough. So he'd go up an octave. It never worked, but working his lungs made him feel like he'd won. Sometimes Squeekie changed his accent and voice while talking to people to see if that'd help them understand him. It never helped, but that didn't stop him. He talked and talked and talked. Eventually he meowed and talked to himself since the people never responded to him in cat tongue.

That's why when the human kittens came in Squeekie tried to talk slow and articulate. Human kittens not only played fetch, but they also could talk to him. They shared a mutual trait: the adults couldn't understand them.

It wasn't hard to tell when a young human was forgetting about his friend. Some of the store's revolving cast of cats told Squeekie stories about their human kittens and how the children would grow until they forgot about them. But best friends were best friends no matter how far away they were and that's what Squeekie held onto.

Squeekie knew the second that Henry stepped through the door that he was forgetting. His brown hair had grown quite a bit since the last time he'd been into the store. He was taller too, with his legs starting to lengthen. But it was Henry's brown eyes that pulled in Squeekie first. The eyes stared at Squeekie like he was a long lost toy instead of recognizing him.

Henry kept a tight hold on his mother's hand as they moved farther into the store. Squeekie trotted up to the two of them.

"Henry. How are you? What's new?" Squeekie began. "Do you have any new toys? Want to look at books?"

Henry squinted before his eyes widened. "Squeekie!"

The little boy jumped forward and sat in front of the cat.

"Aren't you a good cat? What a good kitty," Bob's mom cooed before moving away through the plethora of bookcases.

Squeekie meowed before turning to Henry. "Want to play? I got a cool new mouse toy."

Henry shook his head before asking. "Why did I have a hard time understanding you?"

How many kids had Squeekie met in his life? How many kids had Squeekie become friends with? Small, round, long, square, and a rainbow of colors filled Squeekie's memories. Some came once to the store and returned after it was too late. Some came on what felt like daily playdates, embedding themselves into Squeekie's memory.

Not Henry though. Henry was the first kid he'd ever let become his friend and would even venture into best friend territory.

"Well, it was bound to happen," Squeekie said.

"The thing? My memory block you mean?"

Squeekie nodded. He'd once heard his human describe it. Humans had no memories before they were around four and once that part of the brain developed, that was the end.

"Yeah, your brain is growing. Which is good. I wouldn't want your brain not to grow." Squeekie said. "But you won't be able to talk to me anymore."

Henry pet Squeekie. "But I don't want to forget how to talk with you. Or my dog."

Squeekie nodded. "I wish you'd remember, but it never works. My own mother told me that younger humans understand animals better. I don't know why, but you guys see things so much easier and understand it. But if your brain didn't grow like it was supposed to, then bad stuff would happen"

Henry's mom was making this a fast trip. She moved to the counter, placing the books softly on the counter. She looked over at Squeekie and Henry and pulled out a small camera.

"Henry, move over to Squeekie so I can get a picture of you."

Henry looked at his mom, focusing on her words like they were bouncing around in his brain like a pattern instead of letters. Squeekie could tell when they made sense because he smiled and hugged Squeekie close.

Squeekie looked at the camera and yowled. Henry laughed as did his mom and the other adults in the store. Squeekie wanted to cry.

"I don't think you'll remember me the next time you come in," Squeekie said.

Henry looked at Squeekie and he made the processing look where his eyes squinted and his lips puckered out. "What did you say?"

"Squeekie can't talk honey," Henry's mom said. "It was cute when you were small."

Henry rubbed Squeekie's fur and gave him a hug. Squeekie licked his cheek and watched his first human friend walk away.

Squeekie the Bookstore Cat

4

Squeekie and the Kitten

Samantha Coons

I woke up and heard the delighted squeals of the Usual Humans. I yawned and stretched out my legs, and jumped out of my hiding spot behind the counter, expecting to be met with the Praise of My Beauty and the Attention Consisting of Pets and Scritches. However, there was no one behind the counter at all. I blinked a few times and sniffed at the chair that the Usual Humans sit in, but the excited noises were definitely coming from the other side of my domain.

I sauntered over to the counter and prepared to jump.

"This gets harder every day," I thought to myself. "I think they must be making it higher."

I jumped and barely made it, scrabbling over

the ledge. I looked over to where the Cage that is Mine (as All Things are Mine) was.

The Usual Humans were cooing over something. I squinted and saw them. Two little fluffballs scrambling around. Kittens.

"No!" I yelled, but the Usual Humans didn't seem to hear me.

I jumped down and padded over, slipping between the Cage that is Mine (as All Things are Mine) and the Usual Humans.

"Return these Kittens at once," I demanded in my most commanding voice.

Human who Smells like a Dog leaned over and gave me a few pets.

"You want to meet the kittens too Squeekie?" it said.

"No. I don't."

She picked me up, not understanding as they never understand, and held me out to the cage. A little gray fluffball waddled over and poked her nose at me. I hissed, which didn't faze her because fluffballs are too small and dumb to understand clearly.

"Squeekie" Human who Smells like a Dog chided as the gray fluffball cocked her head at me. Dog Human set me back down on the floor and went back to cooing at the kittens.

I prowled away and spent the rest of the day hiding behind the Magical Curtains that only the Usual Humans can enter.

After darkness had fallen on the store that night, I slunk back out to the Cage that is Mine (as All Things are Mine) and yowled my best yowl. The fluffballs peered down from the top of the Cage that is Mine.

"Hewwo?" the gray one said, once again cocking her head at me. The orange one was curled on the floor, and only the tops of his ears were visible.

"Hello, kittens," I said. "I want you to know that you are in the Cage, which is Mine, in the Store, which is Mine, and that all of the Humans are Mine."

She stared down at me.

"Will you pway wif us?" she said.

I went back behind the Magical Curtain until morning.

Despite explaining over and over again to Mother the next morning why it was a terrible idea to keep kittens in the Store which is Mine, they remained. I did my best to ignore them, they were only kittens after all, and I suppose it was not their fault that they were only kittens. Sometimes Mother talks about when I was a kitten, but if I really was a kitten, I'm sure I was very exceptional.

These kittens were not very exceptional. The gray one ran around the Cage that is Mine playing with anything that would move, and the orange one hid in the Cave of Wondrous Warmth (which I hardly need add, was Mine). The gray one would call out to me and all of the other Cats that are Not Kittens as we went past the cage. We all ignored them, except for Fuzzy Gray who is young enough that he doesn't understand. The Usual Humans and the Humans that Come and Go still paid the fluffballs a lot of Attention that Should Have Been Mine, but within a week they were giving me an acceptable amount of Praise of My Beauty and Attention Consisting of Pets and Scritches so things were alright until the kittens went away (as All Cats who are Not Me go away).

The gray fluffball went away after another week, tucked away in what the humans call a cat carrier being carried by a young duo of smiling humans. I think the cat carriers must be mine, but with so many things that are Mine, it can be hard to keep track. The other Proper Cats and I were glad to see the fluffball go since she was so loud and always called out to us to 'pway' as we went past. Unfortunately, the Going Away of the gray fluffball caused all of the Humans to pay extra attention to the orange fluffball. I watched and patiently waited for the attention to come back to me. After about an hour, I got tired of waiting and went over to the Humans.

"Bad humans, you are supposed to pay attention to me."

Human who Makes the Walls Colorful picked me up.

"Maybe he's lonely. Do you think we should put Squeekie in with him for a while?"

I didn't understand what she meant until I noticed the small orange nose poking out from under a blanket in the cage.

Put me in there? With the kitten?

"I think that's a great idea." Mother called out from behind the counter.

"Mother" I cried, horrified that she was going along with this. I should not have been surprised, Mother is the one who lets these kittens into the store. She is the Greatest and Most Powerful Human, and the one that Gives Me the Most Treats. But for some reason, she likes to have other cats around. I'm still trying to figure out why this is when she has me.

Dog Human opened the latch for the Cage which is Mine, as Mother had spoken and Mother must be obeyed, and Wall Human placed me inside. I meant to try and jump out but was momentarily distracted by the existence of food within the Cage which is Mine, and so when I finally turned back around, the Usual Humans had gone and were doing the Usual Human things. The orange fluffball was still peering from under his blanket. I chose to ignore him and entered the Cave of Wondrous Warmth with my head held high. The kitten didn't bother me.

'Squeekie's Not-So-Inner Monologue: Part 1

It has been so long since I've seen the light
felt the fresh air
stretched my legs and run free
it has now been
...some...
amount of time
since I was put in
but I don't know how to tell time
at least like humans
I am so bored

so unloved
woe to me.'

Before the Usual Humans left for the night, I was released from the Cage which is Mine. Since humans can be tricky and indecisive, I immediately ran behind the Magical Curtain and hid behind a box, because boxes are magical and safe.

It is warm and soft. My mother is in the box with us. My brothers and sister are climbing onto mother, chasing each other. I watch with my newly opened eyes, tucked in a corner. I don't want to close my eyes, but they droop along with my head, and the world is dark again.
Now there are hands. Hands pull out my younger brother, and we don't see him again.
The hands pick me up. I let out a squeak. Mother looks resigned as she watches me go. I keep squeaking. I want to go back.

I woke up, somehow having made my way into the box during the night. I could hear Mother talking to the kitten beyond the Magical Curtain. I thought about jumping out and yowling until she gave me attention or treats, but for some reason, I didn't want to leave the box. It was warm.

'Squeekie's Not-So-Inner Monologue Part 2:

They put me in the Cage which is Mine
with the kitten
again
my life is such agony...'

"Excuse me, sir?" The voice was small and easily ignored, so I ignored it.

'The days become long
and no one pets me
or gives me treats...'

"Sir? Why are you talking to yourself?"
The voice was slightly louder now, but it was asking impertinent questions, so I continued to ignore it.

'Nothing but kitten food
and a small bowl of water
alas
to be have abandoned in such squalor...'

Squeekie and the Kitten

This time an orange head interrupted my refined thoughts. I stopped talking and stared at him. He shrank into himself at that, but managed to pipe up.

"I don't think it's so bad in here…"

I turned around and continued my monolog to the back wall.

I grew to think and take this as you will as I was no doubt severely affected from being trapped in My Cage for so long, that the kitten was not so bad.

He was much quieter than his sister, and he wasn't as pushy. He took to listening to me talk to the Usual Humans as they wander by. He would sit outside the Cave of Wondrous Warmth and nap while they went past and I expressed my displeasure to them, not that they ever listened (being Human and all).

One night after the humans had left, he asked me:

"Will I get to stay here with you and the Humans forever?"

I didn't answer. But I let him into the Cave of Wondrous Warmth with me…which made it even a little warmer.

"The Humans are saying your name a lot the last few days kitten."

"I know."

"And not just the Dog Human. All of the Humans."

"I know."

"That is unacceptable."

The kitten yawned curled up next to me.

"I know."

"I want to know why this injustice must stand."

The kitten didn't answer, either because he was asleep or because he didn't think 'I know' was a proper answer to that statement.

The Dog Human (who had grown annoyingly attached to the kitten) came over and opened the cage to scratch under the kitten's chin.

"Hey little guy...I guess you'll be leaving tomorrow. We'll all be sad to see you go, but your family will be really nice! I promise."

He purred. I don't think he knew what the human was saying.

But I did.

I got up, and the kitten fell to the side, blinking his eyes as he woke up.

I started eating because food is good and never leaves you.

The kitten watched me for a minute before yawning and going back to sleep.

That night I couldn't sleep. I sat in the cage where I had been trapped and stared out at the store without making a sound. Mother would be Proud.

The kitten woke up after an hour or two and saw me sitting.

"What's wrong?" he asked in his Completely Not At All Adorable Little Kitten Voice.

I shrugged.

He stretched and came to sit by me. For a while, neither of us spoke.

"You're leaving tomorrow," I told him.

He cocked his head.

"Leaving what?"

"The bookstore. You're leaving to live with your forever family. Like all the cats do."

He seemed to shrink a little. "Oh."

He shifted his weight from paw to paw for a moment.

"Do you think they will be nice to me? My forever family?"

For a second I was about to say "Probably" but then I saw him beside me, small and quiet. His eyes big and eternally worried looking.

"Yes. That's why you're going there."

He seemed less tense but no less sad after that.

"Mr. Squeekie...you'll always be my friend though right?"

I wanted to scream. I hadn't wanted to like a kitten in the first place. Kittens always go the fastest. I thought this one was different, after being here for so long...but kittens always leave.

"Of course," I told him and started grooming the fur behind his ears.

I watched the next day as his new family came and collected him, how they cooed over him and tickled his feet. The Usual Humans waved goodbye as he was carried in his crate out the door. I saw him watching me the whole time he was leaving. I wanted to close my eyes and try to sleep. But I followed as far as the Humans would let me.

I didn't eat my dinner that night. I lay in the Cave of Wondrous Warmth.

And I missed my friend.

AUTHOR BIOGRAPHY

Samantha Coons writes words sometimes and sometimes they are even good. She edited this book and wrote any text not attributed to another author. She would like you to know all mistakes in this book are her fault. She loves all cats (and dogs and animals) very much.

Squeekie the Bookstore Cat

5

Squeekie and the Books

Samantha Coons

    The bright car lights faded as the humans pulled out of the parking lot. I stood watching them go at the glass door. Annika was running around in the big room, trying to knock treats down from shelves. I would try this as well, but not until morning. At that moment I just sat and watched, and waited.
    After not such a long time I left the door and walked into the dark aisles.
    The books talked to me.
    Perhaps it was not talking in the way that the humans talk to each other. The books murmured to me, it's true, but they also drifted into me. I could feel them, I could feel their stories. Only in the dark, though, and only at night. They would draw into themselves in the daytime when there

are people and noise everywhere and the lights burned down onto the aisles.

The ghosts do that too, but they just hide in the basement, and of course they just talk like regular humans.

That evening I went to my favorite spot - the crafts section in the back room. A lot of sections are noisy and cold, and a creeping feeling will run down your spine, but the crafts section is different. It is soft, like yarn, and warm, and sounds like women murmuring slowly to each other while steel and wood click together. Nearby History is sharp and talks in long, groaning sentences while self-help smiles and chitters, but both are far enough that it becomes a background to my warm nest.

Most nights I went to crafts to sleep. I liked being around people, even if those people were books and the ghosts were mostly in the back room anyway. Sometimes the lady ghost would sit next to me and pat my head while I dozed. I never asked if she could feel the books like I could.

The next morning I stretched and yawned. The books were quieter, which meant the sun was coming up, so I went out to check on Annika and see if she had managed to pull the treats off

Squeekie and the Books

of the counter.

She hadn't, and she wasn't very happy about it. There was a mess of other things on the ground, a stapler, a bunch of slippery papers that I didn't slip on at all, and a few other less interesting bits. She was curled up on the counter and swatted at me as soon as I got near. I pranced away and slid over the counter to the treat bag that was nestled in a cubby. I crouched and pounced, pulling down the treats and a few folded up shirts that were being stored in plastic bags.

I landed gracefully (enough) and looked at Annika. She flicked her tail at me and leaped off the other side of the counter. I didn't give it much thought, I knew that if I got the bag open, she would be back eventually to get her share. I started jumping on the bag with my claws to open it (as everyone knows that is the only way to open a bag).

A few hours, half a bag of treats, and a lot of yelling later I sat on the counter. Mother was watching that screen thing that the humans like to look at, her fingers tapping on the clicky noise machine. A few minutes earlier I had tried to show her how helpful I could be by jumping down and pressing the buttons of the clicky noise machine. Unfortunately, this did not make her less angry about the mess that Annika had made, and she had just pushed me away. So with nothing else to do, I sat on the counter, yawning and dozing on and off.

That was until someone dropped a box of books onto the counter.

I opened my eyes and yowled at the Dog-smelling Human (one of my Store Humans), who smiled and scratched behind my ears. Appeased I stretched and went to smell the box in case it was a good box for sleeping (Squeekie's Note: In fact, all boxes are good boxes for sleeping).

"Are those yours?" Mother asked Dog Human.

"No," Dog Human replied while shaking her head, "They were outside by the door, I didn't want to leave them there."

"Huh..." Mother sounded annoyed.

But something in the box was Not Right. Even during the day books talk to me. Very faintly, but enough that I can tell.

I screeched and jumped away hissing. The humans' heads whipped around toward me.

"Squeekie," Dog Human said in a coo, reaching out. I bolted as soon as she touched me, in case she picked me up and held me closer to the box. I didn't know if it was dangerous, but I didn't want to find out.

"He's been acting weird all day," I heard Mother telling Dog Human, "and when I came in this morning, he had knocked over everything on the counter and torn open a bag of treats."

I ran to the front of the store and jumped onto the table by the window, squeezing myself into the crack there. It was sunny outside, so it was warm, and there were no books on the table to whisper to me. I closed my eyes and thought about what to do about the Not Right.

"Hey!"

I yawned, sneezed, and tried to go back to sleep.

Annika slapped her paw on my forehead.

"Wake up already!"

I yowled.

"You didn't have to hit me…" I said as I stood up and backed away from her.

"You never wake up if I don't!" she snapped, tail swishing.

I backed up a few more inches, just to be safe.

"Well, why do you have to wake me up at all?" I yawned again, noticing that it was dark outside and the lights had been turned off.

Annika lay down on the table, her eyes narrowed.

"I need your help," she said after a long pause. She didn't look pleased to be asking.

"Do you want me to help you get another bag of treats?" I tried not to sound smug, I really did.

"No. And just so you know, the only reason I ate those treats this morning is because I hate to see food go to waste...especially if it's going into your fat mouth."

I stopped licking a paw to pout at her. She ignored my face and continued.

"I need help with a book."

"What do you mean? Did the humans put a bunch of books in your favorite spot? They do that to me all the time..." I sighed as I remember all the wonderful hiding places that had been lost over the years because of books. I lifted a leg to start licking the back of my knee as Annika kept talking.

"No, geez." Out of the corner of my eye, I saw her tail flick back and forth faster. I decided to not to respond yet.

"There's a book that's..." she scrunched up her face, apparently searching for a word, "weird." She finished, her ears flattened.

I stopped licking myself.

"Weird...does it feel not right?" I asked, sitting up straighter.

"Yes, that's what I meant when I said it felt weird," she hissed, but I ignored that.

"I felt that this afternoon when it came in." I said, this time not bothering to hide the smug grin on my face.

She scowled.

"Why are you grinning like that? It's a bad thing."

"Yes," I explained, pausing for effect. "But I knew about it first."

I should have expected the swipe, but I had thought I was out of range. I was wrong, but at least she didn't dig her claws in.

"We need to do something about it." She said as I ran my paw over my cheek to ease the stinging (it didn't really hurt that bad but I thought it was better to make her think it had).

"About what?"

She just stared at me, brows drawing down.

"Oh yes, the weird book. Do you think we can get rid of it?"

She settled down. "Maybe. How would you do that?"

If she was asking me then it meant she didn't really have any idea of what to do herself. I considered, looking out as a bright light flashed by out the window.

"We could take it down to the basement and leave it there," I suggested.

Annika's ears flattened again.

"I don't like it down there...no, I don't think that's a good idea."

I yawned and lay back down.

"We could put it in those big black bags the humans take things away in."

"Maybe...but what if they see it and put it back? And who knows where they take it...what if it ends up affecting one of them?"

I looked at her and smirked.

"I knew you cared about them."

She bristled and looked out the window.

"Well, I mean...they're our people. They give us food and water and..." She shrugged. "Anyway, I don't want to do that."

"We could put it in the big whirlpool fountain in that little room over there. It makes things disappear all the time."

Her ears flicked back up.

"Let's do it." She said.

Unfortunately for us, we didn't know where the not right book was. Together, we walked over

Squeekie and the Books

to the counter.

"So," Annika said, hopping up on the big empty space near the clicky noise maker, "They put the books here first, and then put them on the shelf, right?"

I nodded.

"Then we can find the scent here and just follow it to where it ended up...where are you going?"

I looked over at her from where I sat on the clicky noise machine. "Animal crackers," I said by way of explanation.

She looked torn between batting me again for being off topic and batting me out of the way of the animal crackers. In the end, she slunk over while I retreated to the chair with a cracker in my mouth.

"Once you're done with that you can go get the scent." She said through a mouthful of cracker.

"What? Why do I have to?" I whined.

"Because I said so." Her tail flicked so I stayed quiet...but I still pouted as I took small bites of my cracker to make it last, hoping she might get tired of waiting.

She didn't, so I went back to the counter and put my nose down on the wood. I tiptoed around for a while, catching the scents of different humans and paper and glue. Annika joined me after she had finished her crackers, starting from the other end of the table. We met in the middle. I looked at her.

"Did you smell it?" I asked.

She shook her head. "You?"

I shook my head.

We both sat down and stared at the wooden table.

"I suppose we could each follow a scent…eventually it will have to lead to the weird book." Annika said as she sniffed the table again.

"Annika?" I said.

She looked up.

"What do you think humans do with books?"

She puffed herself up.

"That's easy. They stare at them."

"But why?"

This brought her up short. She turned away from me and began sniffing.

"Probably something about them amuses them. There are all those little squiggles in them. Maybe they think they are a bug or something they can chase."

"What if the little squiggles are actually bugs

that they squished!" I said, brightening up.

"Squeekie," she said.

I looked at her.

"If you go off topic one more time, then I am throwing you in the big water fountain. Now keep smelling."

I licked my paw and waited a minute before I put my nose down and sniffed again just so it was clear that Annika wasn't the boss of me.

In the end, we both found smells strong enough that we could follow where they had gone. One book must have had some coffee spilled on it as it smelled quite strongly. Annika found a cat smell to follow. She went off towards the back room while I followed the smell to the mystery section.

The paperback mystery section isn't as unsettling as the hardback mystery section. In hardback mystery, there is always the sharp scent of blood, voices mumbling quickly back and forth, and a lot of rain. Paperback mystery has a few hints of that, but also female humans gossiping and cats.

Lots of cats.

A female calico stares down her nose at me while a few fluffy kittens and an old dog block the aisle.

The cats from the books aren't like the ghosts. They are farther away and they don't seem to know they are in a bookstore. They only notice me (or Annika) when we come close. One told me once that she worked in a post office and she could see her person behind me (there was nobody behind me, I checked). I think they come out of the books just enough to see us other cats. Of course, humans can't make it out of the books that much, but that's hardly surprising.

The calico was still staring as I sniffed around to find the coffee-smell book.

"What are you looking for?"

I ignored her. I had seen her before, and she wasn't very nice. She said I looked mangy and didn't believe me when I told her about the bookstore, and she hissed at me after I jumped up and knocked over the book she was balancing on to prove we were in a bookstore.

I sniffed over to a shelf and found the coffee-smell book. It smelled very edible, so I licked it once. It was not. I sat back, not sure what to do now that I had found my goal.

The calico laughed.

"If you are looking for that awful thing that was hanging around earlier, you are looking in the wrong place."

I jumped and stared at her then remembered that I was better than her, so I sat and regarded her with a cool eye.

"Something awful went through here?" I said. "You mean, something worse than you?"

She didn't seem phased by my insult, but I was still proud of myself. I'm sure she was just good at pretending.

"It was one of those paper things that your shadowy humans carry around...made my fur stand on end." She licked a paw delicately.

"Is this...thing still around? You know, so I don't run into it by accident."

She smirked.

"No...but I heard someone yelling about it in French afterward."

I had to think for a minute.

French...French would be in language? No, I walked past that section to get to the food, I definitely would have noticed the not rightness, so....

"History!" I yowled.

"You're welcome." The calico said as I ran away. I wasn't even offended by the smugness in her voice I was in such a hurry.

"Annika, history!"

She jumped a foot into the air as I ran past yelling at her. She hurried out of the Collect section and galloped after me.

I turned a corner and came skidding to a stop at the Wall of History. I stared.

Annika trotted behind me and started walking the length of the section, her eyes narrowed.

We both inspected each bookshelf, our fur standing on end.

"It's..." I said as my head tilted to one side.

"Not here." Annika finished. She glared at me.

I would have to go back and knock the calico's book into the magical fountain before we throw the not right book into it.

"Excuse me chaps."

Annika and I both swiveled back and forth, trying to find who had spoken.

"Up here." The little voice said.

We looked up. A little bird with a red breast sat on a shelf a few feet above us. Annika immediately went into a crouch, her eyes fixed on the creature. I batted her ears, and she relaxed.

"We can't eat him...he's still moving," I told her.

Her tail flicked, the dirt flying up in clouds.

"He's still moving...right now..."

The bird cocked his head and flew a few shelves higher.

"Anyway," I said, "he's a book bird so he probably doesn't even taste good. Probably tastes like glue."

She relaxed a bit more, her nose wrinkled.

The bird gave a nervous laugh.

"If you chaps are done talking then, I'm Robin. I end up in this weird place sometime and I seen you around a bit. It seemed like you two were looking for something just now, and there was a book or summat here earlier that seemed a bit strange. Is that what you was looking for?"

Annika seemed stunned that the food was talking so much, so I hurried to answer before Robin kept going.

"Yes! There was a book that came into the store earlier that was not right. Do you know where it is?"

The robin nodded energetically.

"Yup, that's the one bud. 'Cept it went off like a shot earlier after some creepy crawly found it. Scared the burjeezers out of me and my mates."

"Which way?" Annika said, crouching down

again.

Robin gulped and pointed a wing behind the bookcases. Annika was off like a shot, and I hurried behind as Robin chirped and puffed his feathers out in alarm.

Annika came to a halt at the entrance to the stairs. I sat beside her and watched.

Now, the basement used to be a Very Bad Place with a Very Bad Thing living in it. But the Very Bad Thing went away, and now the basement is more of a Very Damp Place more than anything. But some squigglies still live down there in the corners. They are rude more than anything else, and sometimes they can even be fun to chase around. They don't come upstairs.

Well, they don't come upstairs much.

There was a large belch, and a damp book page came flying up the stairs. It floated to the ground right before us.

There was still an air of Not Rightness to it...but most of that seemed to have been washed away by what appeared to be squiggly drool, and there was a large bite mark that marred the top corner.

"Well," Annika said.

I nodded.

Squeekie and the Books

She puffed herself up.

"Grab that page. Something is going in the magical fountain tonight."

I yowled a little in protest, but she batted my nose so I carefully picked the page up in my mouth.

"And then you can get me more treats." She yelled as she pranced out of the room.

I sighed around the mouthful of paper and monster spit. At least I could get a nice long refreshing drink from the magical fountain.

Squeekie the Bookstore Cat

6

Squeekie and Michelle

Samantha Coons

'Mom!'

Mother kept tapping her fingers on the clicky noise machine.

'Mooooom!'

She glanced at me, rolled her eyes, and continued clicking.

I thought that she might listen to me if I was helpful, and made more of the clicky noises for her. I jumped down in front of the screen onto the buttons.

"Squeekie!" she shrieked, "Oh my gosh, get out of here!"

Apparently, I had not made the correct clicky noises so I jumped back onto the tall black box to lay down again.

Sometimes Mother does not pay attention to me, but that is okay because she is Mother.

It's not that I don't enjoy the big building, with all kinds of new and interesting things to find and play with. But where was my red-haired person? She is My Human, and I should not be away from her for this long.

There are humans here, who pet me and feed me. But they aren't MY Human. Where is she? I worry about her.

I cry all through the night as I look for her through the glass of the window.

Mother was preoccupied at the moment, so I decided to go inspect the other humans. Funny blue-haired human was kneeling and putting books away so I padded over and pressed against her legs.

"Hi Squeeks," she said, patting my head. I purred, but she only patted my once or twice more before turning back to the books.

'Don't stop,' I said, 'More pets!'

She just laughed at my voice. I slunk back to the counter and sat beside a pile of books that Mother was scribbling on.

There are three humans who are here the most. One is smaller than the others, which I think means he's younger. The other two are a man and a woman. The man is very close with my new friend Creamsicle, who is very protective of him. I don't mind, I already have a person. The woman seems to like all the cats, and she gave me an extra treat yesterday.

"Do you miss your person?" She asked me. I said yes. She picked me up and held me for a while. She smelled like books and cats.

I had wandered away again, this time, to peer through the glass door of the store. Humans came through it all the time, and humans were good because they paid attention to me.

Sure enough, a few minutes later an older woman came in and cooed at me.

"What a pretty cat! Back away from the door though, go on."

She wouldn't come through the door while I sat there so I backed up a few feet. She came in and started petting me.

"Sorry about that." I heard Mother say through the opening by the counter, "He really isn't supposed to be out there."

The old lady smiled at her and went on her way to look at books.

"I'll get him." I heard Blue-Haired Human say.

I looked around to watch the old woman and was met with a squirt of water. I ran behind the candy machine to hide, but Blue-Haired Human crouched after me and hit me with more water.

This time, I ran out and sat by a bookshelf to clean myself off. My Humans are always shooting water at me when I try to greet people, but not when I follow the people around and talk at them. Humans are funny like that, I guess.

I think that maybe my person isn't coming back. I don't know how long it's been, but other cats have come and gone by now. I want my person, I want to talk and play with her in her warm bed, I want to see my friends the dogs again.
I cry out that night. But there is nobody to hear me.

The old lady resumed admiring me when she came up to the counter.

"He is such a pretty boy." She cooed as she ran her fingers through my fur.

I purred my contentment. Every once in a while, a human will come to the store who does not appreciate my beauty and grace, but for the most part, the people understand that I am an exceptionally exceptional cat. One that is much more interesting than other humans and even other cats.

Of course, as wonderful as it is to be praised for being me, there are things that are more important at times. The woman's bag sitting innocently on the counter, for instance.

I sniffed a corner before sticking my head into the bag. I could hear the old lady giggle at me, which I usually do not like but right now I am exploring. Bags are caves of warmth and new smells. Bags are the best thing in the world.

Hands caught me before I could get my paws into the soft leather.

"Mooom," I said as I was lifted back onto the counter.

She ignored me.

"Do you want to come home with me?" The old lady said with a smile.

Mother stroked my back as she matched the woman's smile.

"He's not up for adoption."

I have a spot for myself in the bookstore where is it nice and warm. It is a big black box that the woman sits next most of the time as she moves her fingers over a bumpy black box. The bumps on the bumpy black box make noise when her fingers move over them. It is kind of relaxing to sit and listen. Every once in a while she will reach up and scratch my head. I think she is my favorite.

I heard the sound...

The sound that meant "Come here Squeekie,

come to me"...

The sound of treats.

I ran to the counter where Mother was shaking the container. There was another person there but that doesn't matter.

Annika was also there, which mattered a lot because she really likes food. She likes food more than she ever liked me, but I try not to be bitter.

She was already munching on a treat, so I was fairly sure that my first treat would be safe at least.

Mother put a few down for me as the other person at the counter pet me. I ate two or three before Annika shot over and gobbled down the rest. I knew better than to complain at her.

Mother picked her up and set her on the floor, then slipped a few more treats to me.

"Who's a good boy?" she said.

The bookstore is my home now. There are lots of places to hide and play, many cat and human friends (and ghosts as well), and lots of treats. Sometimes I still miss my red-haired person, and I hope she is alright. I wonder if she misses me...of course, she must, because everyone here tells me how wonderful I am. The bookstore woman makes sure that everyone knows.

I wonder if she would like to be my person now?

Mother and the little one (who is not so little anymore) say goodbye to me as they turn out the lights and leave. Annika ran off before the door closed behind our People, so I was all alone.

I would say that I never got used to nights at the bookstore, except it's not true. Nights are still the worst part about living here, being all alone in the dark corners with nobody to tell me I'm pretty, but it's not like I was never alone with my red-haired person. She went away during the day all the time...and I didn't have another cat or any ghosts to talk to.

Tonight I think I will try to convince Bob the Bookstore Ghost of my superiority so he can tell me I'm pretty. Night might be a little nicer that way. I used to cry a lot at night, but nobody would listen to me, not even the ghosts. They would avoid me when I was really noisy. So I learned to calm down by watching the bright lights speed by the store and the weird animals that live outside.

I noticed a pale light drifting out of the back, and trotted back towards it, squeaking out a greeting.

I have a name for the woman.

Most humans don't get names, at least in the way humans think of them. The way I recognize humans it through a combination of sight and scent. Sometimes I will refer to a human as Blue-Haired Human or Dog Human, but this is entirely for the humans benefit as they probably would not understand my way of identifying them.

Anyhow, the woman has a special name and one that translates very easily into human-speak.

Mother.

My attempts to persuade Bob were unsuccessful, but he did sit with me and listen while I told him all about the humans who came into the store the previous day. It was nice, although I still wish he could pet me or give me treats. When light began filling the room, Bob began to fade a little and said that he should find a spot for the day (he doesn't like to frighten the humans).

So I waited by the door with eager eyes and watched the little yellow box pull up. Mother got out and smiled as she unlocked the door.

"Morning Squeekie. Who's a good boy?"

7

Squeekie and the Ghosts

Michelle Haring

All night long I talk to the ghosts, and they refuse to answer me. In my first home, my person left me all day with only the other animals. My person tried to sleep in the house at night. I talked to my lovely red haired person all night long. I told her about my day and what I did with the less important animals. Sometimes she listened and replied. Other times, she said, "Shut up, Squeekie" or asked "Do you never shut up Squeekie?"

I knew this meant that she wanted me to be quiet, but I needed to share my day with her. I was so lonely all day long. Then one day she put me in a carrier and brought me to the large building with different sounds, smells, and animals. The floor felt different on my feet with no carpet to cushion me or for me to scratch. There were other cats, but they told me that they are just temporary. This is a place to stay until you find the magical forever home. I do not understand. I have a forever home, I do not belong here.

This place is strange because people are here all day long and different people come and go. It is like the weekend but better than the weekend. It is like a weekend party. So many people talk to me and tell me that I am pretty. It is amazing. The day is not lonely at all. Then the night arrives.

The people tell me goodbye and turn off most of the lights and leave. The other cats state that the solid people depart every single night. The night belongs to the transparent people who are cold and quiet. The transparent people do not talk to me. They drift away when I try to tell them about the day with the solid people. I wonder why I do not see the transparent people when the store is full of solid people. I think it might have something to do with the lights.

When the solid people leave, they extinguish most of the lights. The semi-darkness changes the way the new place appears but also the way that it smells and sounds. At night, the

Squeekie and the Ghosts

bookstore belongs to the ghosts and the cats. I know the people that I can see through are ghosts, and my new home is a bookstore.

My former person told me that I was going to live in the bookstore with her friend. She said that I would be the bookstore cat, and everyone would love me. She did not tell me that I would be alone at night or that there would be ghosts. I am attempting to figure out the etiquette of being the bookstore cat in a haunted bookstore. The days follow the pattern of my first day with attention and love offered by most of the people. The nights are the mystery that I need to solve. How do I convince the ghosts that they can trust me and tell me their stories? I want them to listen to my stories, but I enjoy active and engaged listeners.

First I will count the ghosts. There are three, two males and a female. The ghosts do not seem to interact with each other. One of the ghosts, the malevolent one, does not leave the cavernous, damp basement. He also does not always look like a person. Sometimes he elongates his limbs and reaches around the top of the stairs with arms that resemble tentacles. I am curious about him, but I do not really want to be his friend. He frightens me.

The female ghost looks incredibly sad all the time. Sometimes there are tears running down her face, and other times she wraps her arms around her middle as if she is trying to keep herself together. Her dress is tattered, and her hair is unkempt. She avoids the basement and runs her hands over the spines of the books. Occasionally, I will catch a look of longing on her face as she stares at the shelves.

The other male ghost is my favorite of the three. He appears to be neither sad nor angry, rather he looks resigned to his fate. He wears a hat and overalls with a long sleeved shirt. Sometimes the middle section of his body disappears, and then I see him pull himself back together. He patrols the building at night, and he often stares out the front window with me to watch the trains.

The temporary cats have no opinion on the ghosts, but the temps do not really care about the solid people either. The cats tell me their stories, but I find animals a little bit boring. I prefer people to animals. I am also a fan of mysteries, and the ghosts are the ultimate mystery of my new home. I think I will pick one of the apparitions and make him my communication goal. Perhaps if I follow the train watching ghost all night long for several nights, he will acknowledge me.

I am so frustrated at night because I cannot connect with him. The barrier between the worlds is too thick to traverse. After days of trying, I find a wonderful way to talk to the ghosts so that I know they can hear me. Now we can communicate. It is the magical herb that a day dweller brings to spoil me. This first time, it is inside a lovely cloth pillow which I take and hide. I hide my treasure because even during the day it helps me to hear the ghosts moan and I know they see me. During the day, it is too hard to talk to my fascinating ghost. The solid people keep petting me.

I love catnip because it takes me to a slightly different reality. When I am flying on catnip, I can understand the ghosts, and they can understand me. I know when I access my hidden stash tonight, I can begin to learn his story. The first night the catnip helps me to talk to the ghost.

First, I ask, "What is your name and what is your story?"

He says, "I am Bob, the bookstore ghost. I knew that working on building the railroad would be so much better than working on the family farm. My family was large, and as one of the middle boys, I was an extra at home. I was a big boned farm boy, so when I heard that they were building the Rockville Bridge in 1900, I applied. I was 16."

I interrupt Bob, and I ask, "What is the Rockville Bridge? I do not see a bridge from my window."

Bob says, "The Rockville Bridge is beautiful. It is the longest stone arch and concrete bridge in the world. It is about three miles from here, and people come from all over the world to see it. There is also a book about it. The author signed copies when the bookstore first opened. That was before there were any pesky cats here."

I look at him intently when he says the phrase pesky cats, he cannot mean me. I am an awesome cat. Plus I sense that he wants to tell me his story.

"How did you travel the three miles from there to here?" I ask.

Bob says, "I kept my job with the Pennsylvania Railroad after the bridge was finished. I moved with many of the other general workers to haul stone and dig as the Pennsylvania Railroad built a freight classification yard in Enola, Pennsylvania.

Squeekie and the Ghosts

When the Pennsylvania Railroad finished the Enola freight yard in 1905, I worried that I would lose my job. My job skills were moving stone and dirt. However, I was young, strong, and hard working. These were the only qualifications that the railroad bosses cared about in employees. I started moving freight from one car to another car.

Working on the railroad was strenuous with long hours in all weather conditions. Like most of the single employees, I lived in the bunkhouse near the rail yard. After five years, I was promoted from laborer to brakeman. The job of a brakeman was more skilled than a general laborer, but it was also much more dangerous. As a brakeman, I risked my limbs and my life everyday manipulating the link and pin mechanism and stopping trains with the manual brakes. I knew men that died under the trains and between the trains because all it took was one slip while coupling the trains.

The only people with whom I interacted were my coworkers. I volunteered for the hardest shifts including the overnight shift so that I could keep my job. It was really all that I had."

Bob becomes quiet after this confession. Bob's words make me sad because I hate to be alone. I love people even if they sometimes cannot understand me. I do not comprehend how people can be so lonely. They should connect with other humans because they have voices and can talk all the time. I talk and sometimes people respond to me, but since the day people do not speak cat, the conversations can be rather one sided. It feels like this is a good time to leave him alone because he looks so sad. Plus my catnip is wearing off, and he is becoming fuzzier.

The next night, I jump into the conversation because clearly Bob became a ghost somehow, and I really want to know how this occurred. It may be rude to ask people how they died but I am a cat. I can be rude if I want to be rude.

I ask, "How did you die?"

Bob says, "One night in the winter of 1913, I made my fatal mistake. I got caught between two trains while operating the link and pin coupling. That night was so cold that I had been worried about losing a finger to frostbite, but I lost my life to the trains. My accident gave me a lot of time to think because I was caught between the two trains and the link and pin mechanism trapped me in place. I was actually impaled by the pieces. The type of accident was always fatal, but I would not actually die until the cars were separated. My foreman came to ask if there was anyone that the company could bring to ease my passing. I knew that there was no one that they could call to say a final word to me. I had always been so alone."

At this point, I have to interrupt him again. I want to understand him. His life story and his death story are part of him. However, I really want to know why he is here in my bookstore.

"Do all people who die become ghosts?" I ask.

Bob chuckles at this question.

Bob says, "That is a silly question. There would be so many ghosts surrounding you all the time if that were the case. I believed that I would pass on to something else when the cars separated but I did not. I think that the fear of the next station in my life led to the next part of my tale. When the trains separated, I saw my body fall, but my soul only drifted. I was not free, I was still trapped on earth. I could drift around the yards. I was a ghost. My ghostly range was about an acre. As a ghost, I saw other men die in the rail yards and I saw their souls disappear. I stayed in my acre plot. There were one or two other railroad ghosts but communicating with other ghosts was nearly as difficult as communicating with humans. I quickly learned that human railroad workers really did not want the ghosts to remind them of their own mortality. Many crosses and rosaries had been waved in my face and sometimes thrust into my body."

I said, "The railroad yard is across the street."

Bob said, "I got bored in the Enola Yard. In 1920, my afterlife changed. Within my acre prison, a Plymouth car dealership opened. This meant that I could haunt an actual building. The elements never bothered me because I was a ghost. However, after seven years of circling the yards and watching the technology change, I became bored. At the Plymouth dealership, I learned about cars, and the people that bought them. Plymouth was the Chrysler Corporation's entry into the low-cost car market dominated by Ford at that time. In 1930, the road between my rail yard and my car dealership elevated, and the dealership owners had to build a second level. Half of the building became buried by the construction. If you go into the basement, you can see the plate glass windows that got covered in brick so the original lot could be backfilled."

I say, "I do not like the basement. It is so creepy, and I do not want to talk to whatever lives down there."

Bob says, "The ghost that lives down there has allowed his bitterness to change him into something unpleasant. He does not bother me because he cannot scare me but it is probably best if you avoid him for now. He might come around some day. Here is a good ending point for tonight. I will talk to you more tomorrow if you can score some more catnip."

The next day at the bookstore seems to be so long. I sleep in the front window. I play with a few children. I sleep on top of the computer tower and walk across the keyboard. It is so much fun to make the person typing yell. Finally, it is night time again.

I sit in front of Bob and cock my head to the side. Clearly, he wants to tell me more stories.

Bob says, "As time passed, car dealerships became larger and needed more land than the relatively small footprint of my car dealership. In the 1960s, the Plymouth dealership closed to be replaced by Earl Schieb's car painting business. This business was part of a chain that painted cars for a very low cost. I loved to watch the employees because they did not take themselves very seriously. The employees had fun at work and occasionally in the lower level of the building when the business was closed for the evening.

Sometimes I could interact with the employees that were in the basement after closing because of the special substances that these employees used to party. I also moved their tools and paperwork during the day to alleviate my boredom. In 1970, there was excitement in my building again as the idiots burned the cinder block building to its walls. No one was injured in the fire so no new ghosts joined me after the fiasco. I watched fashion and technology change over the course of the twentieth century. Car paint improved, and there was less need for a car painting business. When Earl Schieb closed, a boat sales business replaced it for several years. After the boat business disappeared, the bookstore appeared in its place."

"Do you like the bookstore?" I ask.

Bob says, "I love the bookstore. The bookstore owners brought a toddler with them and began to fill the space with books. I never had time to read as a human but in my 90 years as a ghost, it filled the time. I honed my reading skills on customer files that employees left open at the car dealership. I worked at manipulating the physical world but my main skill was knocking over piles of paperwork at Earl Schieb. The paperwork was not incredibly interesting but it was words. At the bookstore, I wish that I could open the worlds in the all of the beautiful books. I can read all of the titles. At first there were twenty thousand titles Within five years of the bookstore's opening, there were over one hundred thousand titles that I could read. A family owned the bookstore, so for the first time in my existence, I watched a child grow. When the family moved into the bookstore, the child was two years old. Over the next seven years, I observed the small boy child mature. Then the cats started to appear."

I squeak in excitement because I think that I am about to enter the story. I like listening to stories, but I really like to star in them, too. I forget about the temporary cats. I talk to them, but they do not seem to try as much as I do. I am the first to care about the special properties of the cat nip. They just talk about when they find their new owners.

Bob says, "You were not the first cat to come here. There were cats here for three years before you arrived. No cats tried to be my friend before you. I did not want to scare the bookstore people because I did not want them to take the books away from me. So I have been relatively quiet for the past ten years. I have told you my story for the first time in life and my afterlife. I think we will be good friends now."

Bob's statement makes me very happy. I like new friends. I know the bookstore owner likes me. She tells me that I am the perfect bookstore cat, but now I have a nighttime friend too.

AUTHOR BIOGRAPHY

Michelle Haring is the co-owner of Cupboard Maker Books. She loves all cats but especially Squeekie. She reads approximately a book a day but writes much slower than that.

Squeekie the Bookstore Cat

8

Squeekie and Annika

Michelle Haring

I understand every word that humans say to me and about me. Most other cats also have this ability. Unfortunately, most humans cannot comprehend cat language. Some cats pretend that they do not even hear humans speak. Ignoring human commands is very freeing for cats. If humans knew we understood their demands, they would expect us to obey them. Obedience is not a trait that cats want to adopt.

All day long, I hear my personal human, Michelle, the bookstore owner tell customers about me.

She says, "This is Squeekie, the bookstore cat. He loves attention, and he thinks that all of the people come to the bookstore to see him. He is incredibly sweet and patient even with children.

This is the perfect place for Squeekie because people come to see him all day. He really likes it when people tell him he is pretty."

I internally preen every time I hear these compliments. This secret knowledge of human speech can be painful for some cats. Not every cat is in their ideal home. For the temporary cats at the bookstore, comprehension could be particularly painful. The bookstore cats at Cupboard Maker Books exist in a two-tier system. There are permanent and temporary residents. For years, I have been the permanent resident. In addition, between two and four cats foster in the bookstore until their adoptions. I train the new cats to never leave the building. I also try to caution these temporary cats to never bite or scratch the customers. The kittens rarely stay very long, but some of the adult cats waited for years to find their forever homes.

When two of the temporary cats remained in the bookstore for nearly two years, the dynamic evolved. Both cats had m names, Mac and Matilda. Mac was a cat of exceptional size who had a delicate digestive system. He needed special, bland food or his stomach issues made him extremely grumpy. Once the humans determined his problem, the treats disappeared for over a year. Michelle told everyone that it was not fair to give me treats because he could not eat them. Before his time in foster care, Mac experienced many adventures. He told me about them after store hours. While the store was open, he mainly slept. Mac claimed several special customers who espoused a love of large cats. The special diet and his disinterest in most humans stalled his adoption. On the other hand, Matilda attacked customers.

Matilda was a small black cat with one white spot on her chest. She feared humans and only approached people the first time because of starvation. She lived feral and free for her first year. Freedom for Matilda meant hunger and the malnutrition kept her small. One very cold day in November, she was starving, and a human opened a door to retrieve their own cat who was allowed on outside adventures. Matilda knew that she would not survive the night if she did not eat. She ate, and she appreciated the warmth of the heated house. However, the cat who owned the humans told her that she could not stay, and his people agreed with him. The next day, Matilda entered the foster cat system. Matilda did not like other cats, and she did not particularly like most humans. Her dainty size helped her adoption chances, but her disposition hindered her adoption chances. Sometimes other cats bullied her which made her more solitary. Upon her arrival at the bookstore, she hid in the basement and back room for several months.

During Mac and Matilda's tenure at the bookstore, other adoptable cats came and went, but those two stayed. I began to believe that we would all become permanent bookstore cats. The three of us were not friends, but we were not enemies. We were roommates in a really large space. Then after nearly two years, both Mac and Matilda were adopted within about two weeks. I did not think that I would miss their presence. They were replaced by other temporary cats. I would begin to trade life stories with these new cats. I would teach them the ropes of being a foster bookstore cat, and they would disappear quickly. I was alone for the first time. Before my bookstore life, I had two other cats and sometimes a dog, this loneliness quickly became unbearable.

In spite of the fact that humans cannot understand my language, Michelle noticed the physical changes. All of the food was now for me, and with Mac gone the good food returned. Treats came back too. I still began to lose weight, and I started to chew my fur as a distraction. Michelle no longer told the customers that I was a pretty boy, she now simply said I was a sweet boy. I overheard conversations about my emotional pain and worries about how to help me. This made me feel guilty for causing them to worry. It was a whirlpool of emotional pain.

One day in early June, a police officer appeared at the store. I investigated his presence and listened to his conversation with Michelle.

He asked, "Do you know Betty?"

Michelle said, "Yes, she is my next door neighbor. Is she okay?"

The officer said, "She is being taken to the hospital. She is terribly ill. She will not be returning. Her only concern was her cat, Annika. She told everyone who would listen that you promised to take the cat."

"Of course, I always promised her that I would keep her cat if something happened to her. I am happy to rescue Annika. Is there anything that you need me to do?" she asked.

He said, "We will have animal control catch the cat and bring her to you today."

Within the hour, the frightened, fluffy cat

arrived in my store. Until Annika's arrival, out of seventy-five temporary cats that came through my doors, only two had long hair. Michelle always told people that she loved fluffy cats, and she would have a harder time letting them go. Therefore, she preferred adoptable short haired cats. Annika's terror and confusion rolled off her in waves. Until that day in June, she had only ever met a handful of people when Betty brought her out of the house to see Michelle or the postal carrier. Suddenly in an hour she encountered a larger number of humans than she had seen since her adoption five years ago.

I had been losing weight because of my loneliness. Annika was so thin that I could see her ribs under her shaved sides. She sported a kitty mohawk and resembled a ferret. However, her coloring was gorgeous. She looked like me with blue eyes and beige fur. Her face is much flatter than mine which makes her countenance appear grumpy.

Michelle cuddled the terrified girl and then placed her in a cage. She told the cat that it was for her own protection. That evening after everyone left the store. I introduced myself.

"I am Squeekie, and this is my store. Welcome to my domain," I said.

Annika said, "I have not interacted with another cat since I left my mother and my litter mates. I hardly know how to talk to cats. Of course, I still speak the language. I am not sure if I want to talk to you. I want Betty. I want to go home. It was my space. I had so many tunnels and towers. I could weave between the stacks and hide so many places. Now I am trapped in this jail. I just want to go home. I slept on my own big bed, and Betty fed me from her plate. I do not like this dry cat food or even this smelly wet stuff."

I said, "I heard Michelle talking to the police. It does not sound like your home is an option any more. Michelle promised to take you. You might go to her house or stay here. She talks about her cats at her house, and I know you will be happier here."

All night long, I stayed next to Annika's cage, and we exchanged life stories. I told her about my before the bookstore time when I lived with the pretty lady with the red hair. I told her that I was alone all day with only two other cats. One of the cats hated me, and the other one was really stupid. Sometimes there were dogs, but they went other places too quickly. Annika's life was so different. There were never visitors or parties. In fact, Betty never let anyone else in her house, ever. Sometimes Annika played with the mice, but they did not speak cat or human. There were a few cats outside her windows, but they ignored her calls to visit. I tried to calm her fears about living in a bookstore.

I said, "Being a bookstore cat is a great life. I hope you will be a bookstore cat, too."

It was not love at first sight, it was love at first night. That night of sharing life stories made me wish that I could finally have a permanent partner. I do not think she felt the same way. After talking, it was time for napping, and she cried in her sleep. I could not comfort her because of the evil cage.

She stayed in the cage for two weeks. For a week, every human that tried to touch her bleed from her claws. Michelle also discovered that Betty never took her to the veterinarian. She needed all her vaccinations and the operation. Every single night, I stayed next to her cage until she fell into a restless sleep. She told me about all of the television shows she watched with her person. This was the first time that I heard about Animal Planet. During her incarceration, she and I talked for many hours in the night.

I felt something change after her surgery. During her recovery, she had to stay in the cage for a few days. By this point, Michelle announced to the world that Annika was not up for adoption. She would be a second bookstore cat. I rejoiced. I could not wait to show her all my special places like the catwalk and my front window. We could watch the trains for hours. I would introduce her to my friend, Bob, the bookstore ghost. She and I could cuddle all day. Everyone would say how pretty we both were. I would not be alone again.

Unfortunately, after the surgery, she was different. She did not talk to me at all. She became nicer to the humans. Not nice like me but not overtly hostile. I want her to be my friend again, and I want her to love me. I wish someone would teach me. This will be my quest to win the love of the second bookstore cat. Her mere presence gives me purpose again. I will eat better. I will stop chewing on my fur. I will be beautiful and strong again. I will dance on the catwalks and show her my joy in the customers. I will tempt her to love, and in the meantime, I will be happy.

Squeekie the Bookstore Cat

9

Squeekie and His Friends

Katie Twigg

Squeekie sets his paw on top of the spine and pulls the book off the shelf. He jumps to the side as it tumbles to the floor. Squeekie nudges the book down the aisle towards the counter where there is the best lighting. Leaving the book on the floor he jumps on the counter and works his way up the climbing shelves to get to the catwalk. Over the restroom was Squeekie's secret spot. He picks up a pair of small wire-rimmed glasses in his mouth and carries it back to his book.

His crossed eyes make it tough for him to read so it was complete luck that he stumbled upon them underneath the shelves where all of the children play. They were just his size. He liked to think that he resembled Harry Potter.

But just a bit more feline than typically perceived.

After flipping his ears outwards and placing his glasses just right, he turns to a random page and reads:

Once there was a kitten who had so many toys
Toys for all of the kitten girls and boys
But there were so many he wasn't sure what to do

So instead he hopped around playing with poo

A rattling inside the cage causes him to look up. The new orange kitten is jumping around the litter box frantically playing with something. At first, Squeekie can't tell which toy he is playing with, but upon closer inspection, he realizes that it isn't a toy he is playing with. Surprised, Squeekie glances back down at the pages.

This book can't be talking about the same kitten. Squeekie tells himself. That's impossible. He looks down at the title. "Freeway's Stories."

Squeekie gazes back up at the kitten and calls out, "Hey. What do they call you?"

The kitten watches him for a moment before answering, "Freeway."

Squeekie stares back down at the book again. It's just a coincidence, he attempts to convince himself. He pushes several pages back, heading towards the beginning of the book. Squeekie ends up on a page titled "Matilda's Stories." He immediately begins to read.

Small and black in color. Quiet. Kept to herself. Hid from most humans. Didn't enjoy the company of many other cats. Remained for two years. Until finally—.

More rattling draws his eyes back up to the kitten cage. Freeway is playing around again, this time with an actual toy. But he gets closer and closer to the food and water dishes.

"Freeway." Squeekie tries to warn, but it's too late. Freeway drops the ball into a dish resulting in the water splashing out of the bowl and the cage. The water falls down on both Squeekie and the book.

Squeekie jumps back, startled. His glasses drop to the floor and skid away. The water quickly soaks through the pages causing the ink to run and the paper to wrinkle. Squeekie paws at the pages trying to prevent the water from spreading but ends up catching his claws on the edges and instead tears the pages out of the book.

Suddenly, in a puff of white smoke, Matilda appears before him. More smoke fills the room as Zachary, Jack, Bella, Eevee, and Rubee all appear.

Matilda steps forward, her eyes focused on him. Squeekie can't do anything but stare at his old companion. "Squeekie?" She glanced around sniffing at the air. "Is this the store? What am I doing here?"

Suddenly shrill cries fill the room. The two look over at Eevee and Rubee.

Eevee sits crying, "Where am I? What's going on?"

Meanwhile, Rubee wonders about whining, "What happened to my family? Where's my family?"

Bella walks in front of Rubee to stop her pacing. "Kittens! Stop a moment." She turns to Squeekie. "I want to know what's going on. Why are we back here?"

"I don't—", Squeekie starts before remembering the book. He rushes over to it and flips through the water stained pages. He can faintly tell that the only ruined pages belong to the stories of these six cats.

"Squeekie?" He looks up to find Zachary

Squeekie and his Friends

watching him expectantly.

He tries to explain, "I think it's this book. I found it today and was reading it. Then Freeway," he nods at the kitten watching them from the cage, "he splashed some water that fell on the book, and I tried to clean it up but accidentally ripped out the pages. It was when the pages got torn out of the book that you guys showed up."

"So we're here because of a dumb kitten," Matilda snaps. She glares towards Freeway who backs up from the doors of the cage.

"He didn't mean to," Zachary defends.

Jack calls out, "Guys! We need to get back to our homes."

"Yes we do," Bella agrees. All but Squeekie nod.

Squeekie stares intently at the book. He wonders to himself, "So by ripping out the pages, cats can come back here."

"Squeekie?" Matilda demands, "What are you thinking?"

"I can get my friends back. All of my friends can come back to me." Squeekie flips through the pages and finds "Pumpkin's Story." Then suddenly he swipes out a paw and rips out the page.

"Squeekie!" Matilda yells.

Then Pumpkin appears out of more white smoke. Squeekie barely registers the kitten's confused cries as he searches for more of his friends. When he discovers another story belonging to a friend he tears out the pages again and then Smokey appears before them all.

Matilda is yelling something at him, but he doesn't pay attention. Squeekie is bursting with excitement once he stumbles upon another story that he's searching for.

Another puff of smoke and there sits Mac. "What? Squeekie? What's going on? How did I end up back here?"

"Mac!" Squeekie exclaims running up to him. "I've missed you so much!" He snuggles up to Mac enjoying the feeling of his plump friends' fur. But Mac doesn't snuggle back. He's too busy staring around at the others. "Matilda? Why am I back here?"

Squeekie faintly hears Matilda give some explanation, but he doesn't care until Mac backs away from him.

"So much has happened since you left!" Squeekie states excitedly. "Tons of new people have been coming in with so many new books. I love when they let me sleep in their laps. And a

Squeekie and his Friends

good human brought in a cat tree for me. And there have been so many cats here since you left. And there is a new store cat who stays here with me—".

"Squeekie!" Mac interrupts. Squeekie quiets as he catches his breath. "A lot has happened with me too."

And then they each proceed to tell Squeekie their stories.

Eevee and Rubee practically worshiped their humans. They played with them and cuddled with them and spoiled them rotten. Bella shushes them for they don't seem anywhere finished with their praising.

Zachary and Pumpkin completely adore their human families. They've grown to love them with their entire hearts and don't know what they would do without them in their lives.

Jack excitedly announced that he was no longer named Jack. His forever family named him after some character called Mad-Eye Moody. He declared that his new name is so much cooler than just Jack.

Bella doesn't have many words to describe her adoration for her people. They care for her and don't ask too much of her. They only hope for her to love them and she does.

Smokey can't speak fast enough about his family. They are great cuddlers and feeders and petters and amazing humans. He expresses how much he misses them right now.

Matilda shrugs, "They care about me. They pet me when I want the company. They leave me alone when I want to hide. Their other cat and I get along fine. It's my own space. I don't have to worry about strangers bothering me. It's nice."

A huge smile spreads across Mac's face. "They're great. They feed me, and when my tummy hurts, they just sit and pet me. They're gentle with me, and I love them for it. They always want me to be comfortable. Living with them has been so much fun."

Squeekie brims with excitement, "But now you guys are back to stay, right? And we can bring the rest of our friends back here too!"

"Squeekie," Mac scolds. "You can't do this."

"Don't you get it Mac? We can bring them back. We can bring them all back! We just have to destroy the book. Castle, Sylvester, Smudge, Beckett, Jasper, Creamsicle—".

"Squeekie!" Mac yells. Squeekie pauses a moment, still so excited to see all his friends again. Mac continues, "You need to stop. This is wrong. We can't go and drag everyone back here.

No one wants to be taken from their homes."

"But this is our home," Squeekie cries. He looks around at his friends. "Isn't it?"

"It's your home Squeekie. The rest of us stay here just until we find where we actually belong. Our forever homes."

"But you and Matilda were here for so long." Squeekie tries to convince them.

"Because we hadn't found the right humans yet!" Matilda yells at him.

"How did you know that they were the right humans? How could you tell? You could've been wrong."

Matilda sighs, "I wasn't wrong."

"How do you know?" Squeekie asks.

"I can't explain it. My humans just…" Matilda drifts off into thought. All sit quietly as she struggles to find her words. Finally, Matilda looks back to him. "They felt like home. And they still feel that way to me. I love them."

"She's right," Mac speaks back up. "We love our humans."

Squeekie turns away, not wanting to admit his heartbreak. "What about me? Don't you love me?"

"Of course we do," Mac comforts. "You're my buddy. You always will be. But our families will miss us if we stay. And they take care of us. Just look at the kittens."

Squeekie turns to Eevee, Rubee, Zachary, and now Pumpkin who are sitting together trembling.

Mac sighs, "They're just babies. They want to go home. We all want to go home."

Squeekie stares at the kittens. Their tear-filled eyes plead to him.

They really don't want to be here. Squeekie walks over to Pumpkin and settles in beside him. He snuggles into the small cat's neck knowing just how much he will miss the warmth again.

Squeekie pulls back to peek at Pumpkin's face. "You really love your new family?"

Pumpkin nods solemnly.

Squeekie turns to Smokey. "You won't forget me?"

Smokey gives him a small grin. "Never did. Never will."

"We love you Squeekie," Mac reassures. "We never stopped."

"I love you guys too." Squeekie smiles to himself before remembering the torn up book. "But how am I going to fix this. I don't know how to get you all home."

Jack steps forward. "I think I may have an

idea." They all focus intently. "Let's try putting the pages back into the book. It wasn't until you took the pages out that we appeared here. So if you put them back then maybe we'll be sent back."

Smokey speaks up, "Is there still tape on the counter?"

"Yes," Squeekie replies.

"Maybe we can use that to stick the pages back into the book."

"Good idea." Jack jumps up onto the counter searching around for the tape.

"We should send the kittens back first," Bella states.

They all agree as Jack pushes a tape dispenser up to the edge of the counter.

Mac waddles over to the cat tree placed just inside the entryway. Smokey follows him and together they push it up against the counter. Jack nudges the tape, and it falls on top of the highest level of the cat tree. Jack follows it down, dropping it from level to level to the ground. Then, Mac shoves the tape dispenser over to where the book lays.

Squeekie flips to where Pumpkin's story was and lays the pages back into place. Mac sets a paw on the tape dispenser to keep it in place as

Matilda lifts her paw under the tape and pulls it out and across the binding of the pages.

"I'm gonna miss you Squeekie," Pumpkin mumbles.

Squeekie gives him a small smile. "I'll miss you too." He steps forward and smooths the tape into place, reconnecting the page with the binding of the book.

There's a familiar puff of white smoke around Pumpkin. Once it clears, Pumpkin is no longer there. A few smiles pass around the group, but from then on they all work in silence.

Next, they put Rubee's pages back in place. Then Eevee's, Zachary's, Jack's and Bella's. Smokey snuggles up against Squeekie as they put his pages back into the book. And then there are three.

Matilda looks to Squeekie. "I really do love them. And they love me. I finally found my home."

"I understand. I'm glad you're happy there." Squeekie replies.

"And I did miss you when I left."

"Really?" Squeekie asks amazed.

"Really." Matilda smiles.

Squeekie presses the tape into the book, and Matilda is gone. He turns to Mac and asks, "You sure you won't stay?"

"I've missed you but my family needs me. They would be so upset to find me gone."

"Family," Squeekie mumbles to himself. He looks back to Mac. "Do you think that I'll ever find a family?"

Mac laughs, "Do you really not know? You already have found them." Squeekie watches him with a confused expression. "Everyone who comes here is your family. You love everyone, and everyone loves you. This is where you belong."

Squeekie isn't convinced. "Everyone ends up leaving me, though. Both cats and humans."

"But they never forget you. I can guarantee that."

"You really think so?" Squeekie hopes.

"Why do you think the humans always take pictures of you? It's because they never want to forget you. You make everyone around you smile. That's your gift and this store is the perfect place to use it." Squeekie doesn't say anything. "Just think about it."

Squeekie nods as he pulls out a piece of tape and lines it up.

Mac snuggles up to Squeekie, and for a moment they just sit together enjoying the company.

Finally, Mac speaks up, "I love you Squeekie. You'll always be my best buddy."

Squeekie smiles. "I love you too." He presses down the tape, and the puff of white smoke takes his friend away.

Now Squeekie sits alone, missing his friends all over again.

"What in the world are you doing?" a small voice asks out of the silence. Squeekie turns to find Annika coming towards him from wherever she had been. "You've been making so much noise for hours," she complains. "I've been barely able to sleep."

Squeekie smiles to himself. "Just remembering some old friends."

"Well can you remember them a little more quietly?" she snaps as she walks away.

Squeekie just sits and ponders over Mac's words. Thinking it over, all the humans would light up whenever they would see him. They'd pet him and love him. He suddenly realized that he would miss that attention more than anything in the world. He never would want to lose the love that he receives each and every day.

"Squeekie?" He jumps, startled by the sudden voice. He looks up to see Freeway looking down at him from the cage. He had completely forgotten about him.

Freeway asks, "Those cats really liked their forever homes?"

"Yes, they did."

"Do you think," Freeway wonders, "that someday I'll find a home that I love that much?"

Squeekie smiles at the young kitten. "Of course you will. Every cat finds their forever home someday."

AUTHOR BIOGRAPHY

Katie Twigg is from Lemoyne, Pennsylvania but is currently living in State College as she attends Penn State University. She is a senior, majoring in Digital and Print Journalism with minors in both English and Planetary Science & Astronomy. She aspires to a career as a science writer.

Katie is an avid animal lover who works part-time in a boarding kennel where she gets to play with many different cats and dogs. At home, she loves to spend time with her boyfriend and their pets. In her free time, she likes to read from her ever-growing collection of books that is currently over 1,100.

Katie was previously employed at Cupboard Maker Books for over two years. Those days were filled with passionate book discussions, adoring cats, and tons of fun. She still loves to visit the store, the cats, and everyone there as often as she can.

ABOUT THE AUTHOR

Squeekie is the bookstore cat at The Cupboard Maker Books in Enola, Pennsylvania. He loves treats, people, the foster cats that come through his store, and Annika.

www.ingramcontent.com/pod-product-compliance
Lightning Source LLC
Chambersburg PA
CBHW071005080526
44587CB00015B/2349